The Gate

A COLLECTION OF POEMS

by

Ansel Brown

iUniverse, Inc.

Bloomington

The Gate
A Collection of Poems

iUniverse books may be ordered through booksellers or by contacting:

iUniverse
1663 Liberty Drive
Bloomington, IN 47403
www.iuniverse.com
1-800-Authors (1-800-288-4677)

ISBN: 978-1-4759-6197-3 (sc)
ISBN: 978-1-4759-6198-0 (ebk)

Library of Congress Control Number: 2012921566

Printed in the United States of America

iUniverse rev. date: 11/17/2012

Contents

The Gate

Acnowledgements

The poet wishes to acknowledge the artistic contributions made by Denton and Danny Williams and EVision and Sound Productions, made to the cover designs and interior art-work of this book. He also wishes to express gratitude to the competent staff of IUniverse Inc. for their continued support throughout this project. Thanks also to my parents; Veronica and Hansle Brown for their moral and financial support.

Foreword

"When you search for ways to express yourself, follow your ways and be yourself. For what is poetry? Nothing but your version of reality, and what is art? Emptiness, if the feelings do not come from your heart."

We depart with conviction and soon after, arrive at a place called poetry. A new and exciting world created by our hands and imagination. On a blank page we breathe life. The paper is stained by our artful inscriptions. The marks remain indelibly. Ink; its cause and consequence scattered across our yesterdays that have been converted into lines and verses. This is the dialogue of our existence which is summarized by poetry.

We embrace the pen in a mystical dance, purposeful and figurative. Writing is equivalent to flying, in a human sense. Poetically speaking, we are birds with flight innate and instinctive. Boldly we leap across the latitude of a page; its desolate fields and looming mountains, to chase and capture that grand and illusive dream.

The Gate

The gate opens to
The outside world,
A wondrously wild, wide
Wilderness.
If you would leave its sanctuary
And venture on your own endeavor,
With each step
You drift farther
And farther into
A never-ending dream.

You are awake.
Maybe
You are a journeyman
Free to roam the vast unknown
Domain of your imagination,
Fueled by thoughts
On a quest designed
To get away
From the bondage of the chains,
The insane, ridiculous, and mundane,
That is the wall.
What you desire is
The gate,
But all you do
Is wait
Trapped and cornered
In this prison of a life
You are living.

A Vanishing Moment

I proceed and I progress,
I go south
And I go west.
Hither I am,
A vanishing moment to stay,
Thrown in the wastebasket of time,
The recycled today,
And though I loathe this reality
With such bitter disdain
Across the fields of misfortune,
The sorrowful footprints
Remain.

Time

I have watched time
Grow a fiery bloom on a stem,
Then render it pale
And lukewarm again,
Playing such cruel tricks on petals
Yearning for the burst of spring,
Then gone like most of everything
Carried away in time.

And I have seen
With anxious eyes the eastern skies
Light up,
Alive like many other ill-fated mornings
Calling without an answer,
For time is spent dwelling on sorrow,
Thoughtless of tomorrow,
While sipping idly today
A cocktail brewed with shrewd misconception,
The bitter-tasting reflections that stain
Once-youthful lips
Dripping dewdrop
From adolescent leaves
That leaves for adulthood much too soon
The same unexpressed morning
And that somber, heartbroken afternoon
Reminiscing on things
And time.

Real Estate

In my mind
There flows a stream
To nowhere,
Gently,
Noisily at times,
A constant stream of my thoughts.
There is a meadow,
Green and inviting.
Birds are in the company of trees
And the breeze walks with graceful ease.
You would be pleased
If you owned the real estate of my mind's
Prime property.
My thoughts are vast open spaces
Where wild creatures roam
Far from home
To the edge of existing.
There are no fences,
No roads ending,
No lines delineating.
Doubts and free-thinking prohibitions
Had long been removed.
Seems they
Were never there
In any other caged mind's manifestations—
Not mine,
For in my mind,
There stands a reminder to anyone
Who desires to enter:
No animals permitted.
No trespassing
Nor destruction of property.

For the Sake of Our Nation

Let us put together
Our art
For the sake of
Our nation.
Poets, painters, sculptors,
Expressionists alike
Combining strengths to lift
This fallen generation.

Let us rise
Above ourselves and speak
With our souls.
Voices in harmony,
It's time to regain control.

Fight for redemption!
We all must be free
From envy and hate
And their certain corruption;
We must have that victory

For the sake of our nation,
Men, women, and children—
People of noble intention.

Blueprint

This is
The creative component
Responsible for the birth of new ideas,
The cradle of insight and ingenuity,
An industry for the make and model
Of dreams,
Aspirations grand and large,
The mass production of an intangible product
With methods and machinery,
Works and wheels of a fabled sort,
Ideas conceived in a mind to illustrate
The dimensional structure and vision of
A blueprint.

Perfectly

Thank you
For teaching me
The exploration of myself.
Help me to
Explore myself some more.
Give me the key
For the treasure chest
Within myself.
Give me the strength
To unlock all the doors.
Make me a gem
That I may be proud of myself.
Make me
Perfectly,
The way I was before.

Voice

You speak of meaning,
And leaning forward with confident eyes,
You affirm my faith
In the simple things.
Now I am a listener
Spellbound by your voice's caress,
The effortless way you deliver
A line
Astounding.
And it reads:
"You speak of passions kept,
Desires awakened,
And longings
That had slept."
While doubt was still questioning,
You spoke again
In a clear voice,
And I heard.

For the Want of Paper

For the want of paper
And the need of a pen,
For the simple pleasing words
When they arrive again,

For a walk to the river,
For an idle gaze,
A chance to talk to a flower
And deflect the shimmering rays,

For the love of expressing
And the miracle of a line,
For the skill of conjuring
Poetry of a certain kind.

If Paint Were Words

He would like to inspire
A portrait of himself,
So he writes
Till sky blue and forest green
Drip,
Drop from a paintbrush
Where he stands
Suspecting the canvas,
Inspecting the graceful and
Awkward bristle stokes of masterful
Time that paints him aged.

He would like to retire
To an inn somewhere,
A holiday by a lazy
Sunday afternoon
Spent in solitude slept,
Not cursing colors.

For he would paint
If he had words,
Fight for the privilege of pastures
Like the hungry herds
That gather
To graze the canvas,
Then walk away with bitten
Green leaves and sun-ripened laughter
Falling from overfed mouths.

To Paint, to Smile

Laughter is
Wet paint
Dripping from inception.
The primary theme of painting
Derives that a canvas once bare
Now bears
The images of conception
Where watercolors fall
From a brush
Onto a fabric,
Emotion with its
Compartments of complex layers
Entwined.
The appreciation of art
Inclines a keen eye to find
And pierce the clustered layers
Of tears,
To continue
To paint,
To smile.

Rhyme with Blue

Your pupil is black
Just like my shoe.
Your eyes are bright
And mine are too.
The fire burns
In but a few.
The darkness turns;
The light shines through.
We see
A world of things to do.
The colors of heaven
Rhyme with blue.

Poetry

Who is mad?
Me?
Caught up in explaining this mystery that touches me
Within like a fire
As faint as a flicker,
Then growing in a furnace into
A raging inferno,
An endlessly consuming conflagration of your imagination,
Smiling,
Watching me trying to write and think of poetry.

Who talks?
The silent one who dwells with words,
Listens, and writes?
You?
Gesturing loudly, shouting and living
While you watch me write,
Feel the flame and listen again to
Poetry.

Who hath life in his hands?
You?
Rocking an infant to sleep,
Living in the innocence of
Its eyes,
Or me,
Feeling my soul, the great fire,
Blaze in my bones,
Surge in my veins, and jolt through my fingertips
While I hold the tool I know nothing of?

Remembering this madness and where it all started:
I was once a child.
I grew up.
My dear friends die,
I mourn and cry,
Yet I die within
And feel on my skin
The seasons change
And flowers fade in days of gloom
And relatives perish like a lovely bloom
And custom fly
To days gone by,
And time will change
As we rearrange
Our lives to cope
With this lost hope.
But time is infinity
And this poetry
Of pages turned
And things I've learned,
Of sentence done
And thoughts just begun,
Of madness and rhyme
At the start of this poem,
Of turning the page
To remember the age
When I started to write,
And though it is long,
It had just begun
To tell the tale
Of men who have failed
To speak the truth,
Of a passive youth
Who sat and wrote

A very long note
On a Monday night
Though he shook in fright
And paused to see
You smiling at me.
Then I remembered the moment you said
Stop.
You laughed, but I kept on:
Choosing the words
And using the verbs
To strongly say
I remember the day
When my best friend died
And indeed I cried
When I did not see
Him smiling at me.
Like the fire inside my heart,
The moment I start to write
Poetry.

Now who will talk
As we boldly walk
And turn the page
Of this poem's age
And try to explain

The power in my veins,
And it you have read,
The moment you said
It is wrong to fight
When beauty is in sight.
You must sit in silence and listen as I write,
Smile with myself, and create poetry.

Autonomy

We seek to illuminate
A path that has never been lit,
A hallway to hopeful ideals
And clear understanding.
Our desire is to see
Where we are most blind
And with an aim of discovery
And autonomy,
Small secrets of self and soul
To find.
We ask that today be eternal.
We place a sacrifice
At the altar of this instant
And beseech the gods of now
That the sin-confessed yesterday
And the bitter, unrepentant tomorrow
Shall by design and time
Manifest virtues
Seeking also to find
In the darkness that dwells
Within us
Where the mysteries of self
Are unknown
And the light of the truth
Is hidden.

Where Did I Lose Myself?

Where did I lose sight
Of the sun, the sand, and the rain?
Where did I wave good-bye
When—alas!—
I could not endure the pain?
Where did I fall silently without a voice?
Forced to go against my will,
It was not my choice.
To where did my soul flee
When it could not stay,
Could not stay within me?
Oh, where?
Where did I lose
Myself?

Test Match

The pitch has a little bit of rough
And a fair amount of green.
The bowler is looking rather tough
And is acting very mean.
I'm playing before my home crowd
And I am trying not to fail
As he turns and starts his run-up,
Blazing with fire on his trail.
I was dropped in the gully,
Trying unsuccessfully to hook
The very next delivery of a no-ball.
A spectacular catch the close infielder took.
I went foolishly for a run
That I knew wasn't there.
The nonstriker was fixed at his crease
Waving and shouting with a glare.
I thought if I survived the morning session
I might make it through to tea,
Then I narrowly escaped in the slips,
Edging an outswinger I didn't see.
I played a stroke to a delivery
That I felt wasn't right.

Then the sky darkened in a hurry;
I started to worry about the light.
My foot movement was lacking.
I tried to correct it in the net.
We had lost six wickets
To avoid the follow-on.
There were fifty more to get—
forty-six, in fact.
Adding that boundary to the score,
If we mix defense with attack,
I'm sure we'll get some more.
The captain has gone on the offensive,
Choosing a completely different field.
We can't afford to lose another wicket.
The tail end—it's my job to shield.
But before the over was finished,
A wide ball he tried to drive.
Now the fielders who were asleep
Have suddenly come alive.
The next batsman in is a rabbit;
His deficiencies are too numerous to ignore.
He should be pleased if he gets off the mark.
I would be surprised if he makes four.

The fielders are closing in;
The outcome does not look good.
Avoid a third loss at the start of the test,
I really thought we could.
We lost another wicket and fell closer to defeat,
And as I gazed unto the pavilion, all I could see were empty seats.
Luckily we made it through to tea with one session left to face,
Four fiery fast bowlers on a wearing pitch
With varying bounce and pace.
There were fifteen over to be bowled;
I was not out on thirty-three.
The batsman at the other end,
I told him to defend
And leave the scoring to me.
We battled through till evening
And were unbeaten at the close.
We managed to save the test series
And are now heroes,
I suppose.

Brave

Brave—
Thrusting your heart to the steel
Grave,
Locked in a cold place, cannot feel
Pain;
The sorrowful emotions and the hurt
Rain;
Falling teardrops to the dirt
Cry;
Echoes of anguish in a crowd
Die;
Dream eyes covered with a shroud

Live;
Scattered seeds flourish from the land
Give
To another your outstretched hand
And go
Somewhere peaceful you ought to be
But know
Your special place
In history.

Death

I can tell
You are losing.
You are holding the blade.
To a dark cell
You are going.
You should be afraid.

Your blood is dripping,
Your life
Slipping away.
Your spirit is rising;
Your soul cannot stay.

I can tell
You are trembling.
Your hands are not still.
In a well
You are drowning
Against your will.

The cold is rising.
It's now at your waist.
Your limbs are not moving.
There is a pale look on your face.

I can tell
You are leaving.
Now say good-bye.
Farewell to the bereaving
Death!
It's your turn
To die.

Live until You Die

Live until you die.
Say hello in the morning;
In the evening,
Wave good-bye.

While nothing happens
For the lifelong day,
Sit alone in the sunshine
While the hours fade away.

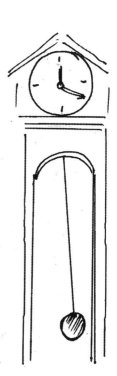

And live until you die.
Enjoy the green pastures
And nature's fruit;
Play with the creatures
In the early morning youth.

'Cause in the evening
The light wears dim,
And while the sun is setting,
The leaf is withering
On the limb.

Live
Until you die.
Say hello in the morning;
In the evening,
Wave good-bye.

Twilight

No one knows
Where the sunshine goes
When she wanders off
Into the evening.
No one cares to see
The dusk appear
While the twilight fades.
At the place where
The day is leaning,
Bright colors change
To gray, black, and white.
The stage is now set
For a date with night.

June Day Departed

And they paused
For posterity
With your vessel
Empty and aloft.
Whispering an epitaph
In their native tongue,
They walked with white
Shroud on high,
A litany to the gods
Of pale evening.
Night is awake
With incense burning
And starlight gleaming
Through torn raiment.
A mourner puts
A withered branch
Into the fire and watches
The lifeless nature
Burn.

They cremated you
At dawn.
At daybreak
And the end of a vigil,
Night departed
And ash remains,
A keepsake
For every
June day
Celebrated.

Last Night

Last night tried to capture me
Deep in the dark,
Didn't want to set me free,
But I had to see today—
Lost in a dream,
I could not stay.
So I fought with all my might.
I knew that dawn would bring a light
And someplace warm
Where I would be feeling the sun
Shining down on me.

Last night tried to steal my soul.
Struggling in the dark,
I almost lost control.
I called out to fate.
Her soft, kind hands
Led me through the gate
The darkness had locked me in
And my day could not begin,
But I rose from the dead
And the dark
Where I laid my head.

Temporal Things

For the future of our liberty
And the freedoms of the past;
For chance that hangs on limbs—
Temporal things
That just can't last—
To the protectors of our sanity
And the keepers of
The gate;
For the meditations,
The methods of balancing
And existing in a peaceful state;
To the balm that knows our healing
And the hand that soothes with a touch;
Through mental storms,
Still we find meaning;
And for these temporal things,
We are thankful much.

I Do Know

I don't know when it started.
I must have
Awakened suddenly
From a dream
As I saw my infantile
Reflection in a stream
On a sunny April
Thursday morning.
My mother realized
And there was joy in her eyes.
It had begun . . .

I don't know when it will end.
Perhaps I will
Return to my dream
When all the water
Is gone from the stream
And the setting sun shows
The last radiant beam
Of sunlight.

I do know how much
I am enjoying it.

You Don't Know Me

You don't know me.
I don't know you.
They don't know us.
But who cares?
Time keeps moving,
Poetry improving,
Slowly months
Replaced by years.
You don't see that.
We can be whatever thing we will,
And though we're trying
To cease the crying,
Tears are falling
Still.

You don't know me.
I don't know you.
We don't know ourselves at all.
Still we remain
A living vein
Till autumn leaves
Fall.

On Sundays

On Sundays
I am usually alone,
Seated somewhere in a quiet place,
A state of mind and a state of things
Left.
Discarded centerfolds of the week's news
Litter the ground beneath me,
Unsettling headlines,
But I am undisturbed
For Sundays are of a relaxing kind:
A time to
Step back,
Think deeply, and, inflect
From things done
Then move on
In the slavish procession
Of Monday.

The Mystical Dove

The mystical dove flies.
It soars from youth.
That ancient tree bears
An adolescent fruit.
We traversed for miles
To get a taste.
The exams passed,
The reports placed
In parents' proud hands,
The teachers' note
Of disciplines adhered to,
Bold destinies we wrote.
We grew in worth
From grade
To grade,
Saying hello to new classmates
As the summers did fade.
Graduation gained on us
When we were least aware,
And before we could gasp,
It was six years.
But the bars we scaled
Are forever held high.
My fair
And beautiful alma mater,
I bid thee good-bye.

There Was a Bird

There was a bird—
I just thought
I'd begin with it.
There was a pond
And after school
We would swim in it.
There was no fortune,
Though fortunate we were
That on those advent days
Real harm did not occur.

There was a place—
I was content with it,
And in the mornings
I would eagerly run to it.

There was a stone
And a limb
On which to sit,
A piece of mind and solitude
That lasted a lengthy bit.

There was a road
That led to the hills
Afar
At a spot where,
If you leaped,
You could reach
The stars.

There was a girl
With red roses in her hair
And a yellow moon on the horizon
That might still be there.

Let Me Go

And let me go
To where I have not gone before,
The nearby new surroundings sweet.
I had not seen such beauty,
Barred from my eyes
Though always within my reach.
But you wouldn't
Let me go.
I am not at peace.
My voice is caged in vaults of silence
More fierce than steel,
And it is real,
The hurt that haunts me here,
Trapped behind these walls of fear.
Let me go!
Let me go!

For Freedom's Loss

For freedoms lost
And liberties taken,
For men forcefully enslaved
And for wills forsaken,
For ignorance and not knowing,
For justices
And injustice is
Destinies locked up
And never going,
For truths be half
And outlooks gloomy,
For sorrow's scornful laugh
And insides insufficiently roomy,
For days asunder
And unseen,
For moments of clarity
And instances of bliss
That lay between,
For thirst and hunger,
For getaways to holidays
And prosperity's blunder,
For deeds undone
And journeys
Not beginning,
For battles not won
And insurmountable challenges
Never winning.

Campsfield House

Are you the new guy?
Allow me to show you what's new.
The house comes with
Bars on both windows.
Each angle offers a different view.
So you are the new guy.
Tell me why
And from where you came.
Please feel obliged
To share your story.
Let us help you
Give your journey a name.

The welcome basket
Is mandatory,
Equipped with toothpaste,
Soap, and brush.
Most rooms have a personal compartment
For the house is built as such.
There will be time to sort
The papers,
To reflect on the route you came.
After a while you will be used to the surroundings.
Sometime soon across loudspeakers
You will hear your name.

This business is official.
You own an identity card
And a new set of keys.
Be sure to visit the clinic
And enter into the records
You are completely well.
You will feel more at ease.

A meal is prepared
Three times daily.
Catch the others
If the first you miss;
Put a banana in your right pocket.
Conceal some illicit biscuits
In your fist.
The keepers are watching closely
If with your toast
You are about to leave.
What you eat in the morning
Must be sufficient.
Dinner is often not what
You hoped to receive.

There are friends for the making.
Foes and fool abound.
There is a convict
In every corner,
A hardened criminal
Who seeks no crown.
Inside, the mood is somber.
Neither wealth nor possession
Of which to boast—
All you have is suddenly taken.
Now it is your freedom
You desire the most.

Plight of Exasperation

Sometimes it takes a while
For your mind to catch up with itself.
It would seem that what is real
Sprinted away into days from now
Where you are already waiting
But not aware,
And in your makeshift room
At the removal center,
Tonight as emotionally exhausted
As you might be,
Still you will have to enter
And crawl reluctantly to sleep
In your bed aloft
And suffer the alien all-night conversation
Of two Middle Eastern detainees'
Plight of exasperation.

Prison Poem

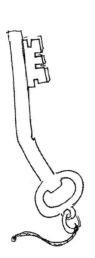

To my friends
And companions
Who are now
Beneath a lock
At the district prison doing time,
Staring restlessly at the clock,
Know that your day will dawn
Just as peacefully as could be.
The instant
You exit
That caging gate
And make it official,
You are free.
The journey never ventured better.
You look back
And to yourself
Read those prison poems.
You once wrote
Yourself a letter:

Dearest me,
I long to see
A mirror
Laid like a leopard
Awaiting sleep
And the simplicity of tomorrow.
My keepers
Have made me weary.
My sentence,
Serving an awful amount.
The space
In my mind,
Confining.
The distance ahead is dreary.
Today more days on a calendar,
I count.

Subjugate

Inferiority is
The chain that binds
The limbs of a weak mankind.
The majority is not yet free.
His thoughts are enslaved
By the force of a greater poetry.

Superiority is
The strength to find
And vanquish
The weaknesses of the mind.
Poets are the few
Who are free—
Free to use thoughts
To escape a caged
Mentality.

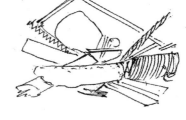

Sugar Mills

Sugar mills, black skins,
Blood and chain,
Men with whips inflicting pain.
Slavery!
Release me,
A lonely human's cry.
Oppression.
Confession.
Many more would die.

Sugar mills, mortal sins,
Oppressive men in control,
Robbing the liberty
From his fellow man's soul

Sugar mills standing
Though the main slavery
Is long dead.
Many bring flowers,
A tribute where they laid his head.

Black man,
Strong man,
Now you are free.
Leave the mills turning behind
Where they belong
On the plantations
Of history.

Inferior

Nothing of substance,
Worth, and strength,
A passive voice is never a choice
For shouting.
The tone is mild,
The footprints vanish from the sand.
You were never here,
Neither alive nor bold.
In the eyes of true greatness
You trembled.
Inferior!
Lacking in might.

The Price

And now whenever I return
To this place
Where all my memories are placed
Neatly in a shopping bag,
And as I pay for the purchased present,
Presently a shopper exits
Bearing a bundle of tightly wrapped expectations.
And what would you expect
For the wages of a fifty-hour workweek
And the joys of a meek minimum wage?
Unemployment brings the maximum
Stress on would-be paydays
When no time can be bought,
No somber mood paid for.
Shopping for sanity
At a rather insane cost on reflection,
A moody manikin marshals the window
Of the store
Where consumers clamor constantly
About the price.

Mystery and Illusion

Mystery and illusion
A bundle of confusion,
Wealth without distribution
Poverty and starvation,
A curse upon a nation
No health, no education—
Unemployment fuels frustration
To rob without hesitation.
The result is incarceration.
You are held at a station,
Given time for contemplation,
Until you reach the realization
You should have surveyed
The situation.

The Truth of Myth and Fairy Tale

I dreamt
That I was more than myself.
In the land of myth and fairy tale,
There lived a greater me.

I awakened aiming to be him,
To inspire myself to live
The vision of a higher being.

Transported beyond my mortal limits
At night in the arms
Of a beautiful flight,

I had a dream.
I was a bird.
I flew to find an angel,
Stood upon its wings,
And viewed eternity.

Theater of the Celestial

With clear and focused eyes,
We appreciate and analyze
The sacredness of the real,
The intricacy of a disguise.

Both night and day
Are driven by a cause.
The sun sits in his seat;
The moonlight savors
The applause.

With pupils dilated,
The audience peers
For a view.
The theater of the celestial
Is now open
To you.

This Great Moment

Please,
Never let me wander
From this great moment.
Keep me poised
While its essence flame burns
Through ages hence,
Kindling and shimmering
With unending glory.
Never let me stray
To destiny's dark vale,
For surely there
I will lose sight of this,
My mortal being,
And never again
Cast watchful eyes
On the blissful light of day

Change and Change

And we watch
As fall's tide slides to the shore
And in that motion so sure
While the world is tilting,
The focus is shifting,
And we change
And change again to remain the same
Till states dwell within us
That we cannot identify,
Ideas and ideals
Now existing
Distant and strange,
The place to which we travel
With cautiously suspecting steps
While a frangible reality through our fingers
Falls
And falls
And fall finds the path back
From frigid seasons
With strange reasons to justify
Changing.

Passed

I have passed
Where yesterday became
Today,
Passed the twilight
And dusk
And still farther away
Beyond night,
Close to the sight of dawn
To where the mist scatters,
Permitting the light of morn
Through the barriers of sleep
And dream,
And hopes awake
To the forefront of eternity.
Another mortal step
I take.

Rage

Beat your drums,
Then pause for silence.
Press a hand against your chest
And hold infinity.
Blow your wind
And go to rest.
Rage!
Rage against sleep
And the dying light.
Brave the dark
Till morning,
Then rise from frozen fields
To find
Me waiting.

Raging Bull

You wave time by
With a red blanket
And pray you are not pierced
By its pointed horns.
A dangerous dance you dare to do
In the arena of harsh circumstance.
The eager spectators have long left,
The final confetti
Falls in silence,
And though you still bear
Those brutal battle scars,
Tomorrow you wouldn't
Live less.

Trying

And
Today you tried,
Leaped for desired heights, and fell,
And it seemed
All in vain
'Cause yesterday
You had tried,
Braved tempestuous seas and torrent's swell,
And trying brought
So much pain,
And tomorrow
You may try,
Trade blows with a defiant fate
To find that
It might not be,
But still you try.
You hope.
You wait.
Someday you will see;
Trying makes you
Hopeful,
Trying though
You are
Doubtful.

Reflections

A sweet symphony of moments
In a day
That still soils the fabric
Of my consciousness
Gently, juices I once
Sipped—
Rare, tasty instances
That slipped from
Youthful, eager lips
And nested on my chest—
Yesterday's sweet stains that left
A tasty trail
On my shirt
And vest.

Penultimate

So I lie there quietly
With my pen in my hand,
My notebook new—
As new as the ink that was now to become it—
While he snores loudly.
Much to mutter about in sleep tonight
For sleep-saturated sounds
May awake the keepers of our fortune
And cause us to walk away
From here
Miraculously, consciously,
Bright, shiny eyes awake and aware,
Not dreaming.

But for now
We lie and lie bare
All our empty, infertile expectations
Of freedom's flowing fountain.
In shackles and chains instead
We are led to bed
Tonight—

Led to believe that morning
May not find us here
Still snoring and unaware
That here,
Where same-fated pilgrims have traveled,
Is no place
To place
Our dwindling life supplies
And camp for the night
Lest wild wolves about us hound.
Pray ye is not made to tremble
By that awful sound
That closing doors make
When sleepy keys amidst them
Turn
And the lights go out in a minute
And in a minute
I too will be asleep,
Wondering
And waiting to see
If this will be
My penultimate night.

The Great Good

The moments arrive
And they go fast.
Hold on as you might;
This one won't last.
Reach deeply for its essence.
There is much to savor.
Spend not your time predicting
Its erratic behavior.
The breath escapes your nostrils,
So you are not through.
As long as the sun rises in the morning,
There is much to do.
Your will and strength
Are the two you give.
Follow through your aspirations
As long as you live.
The mood might change
For the cause to permit
Atrocities against your heart
Harsh circumstances commit.

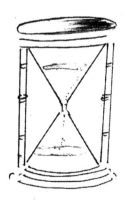

You find yourself in a dreadful place
The instant you arise and the pain you embrace.
Commit your all to the object you seek.
Be confident in yourself and the words you speak.
Find strength in your achievements
And the wisdom you have read.
Take your piece of the pleasure
'Cause you are not dead.
Remember it's all in a moment
And in an instant you go.
Be at peace with nature
And the real things you know.
Let not your mind grow weary
And your heart become cold and sad.
Never let go of the memory
Of the great good you had.